How to Find Whe

Rose Condo is a Canadian poet and educator based in Prestwich, England. She performs her work nationally and internationally, was longlisted for the inaugural Jerwood Compton Poetry Fellowship, has won numerous poetry slams, and performed at the Royal Albert Hall in London. Her poetry show, *The Geography of Me*, won the 2021 Buxton Fringe Spoken Word Award, whilst *The Empathy Experiment* received critical acclaim at the 2019 Edinburgh Fringe and won Best Spoken Word Show at the 2019 Gtr Manchester Fringe. *How to Starve an Artist* was Best Spoken Word Show runner-up in the 2017 Saboteur Awards. Rose was a contributing writer to the groundbreaking anthology *Spoken Word in the UK* (eds. Lucy English & Jack McGowan, Routledge, 2021).

Also by the author

After the Storm

Praise for the author and her works

"*How to Find Where You Belong* is the friend you will carry in your bag. It's the comfort you will seek when questioning your own ability. It's the light that will guide your inner being to realising you can be authentically you." *Sharena Lee Satti, poet*

"A wellspring of genuine emotion gushes from every meticulously shaped piece. There is an organic honesty here, messy and relatable, that many have failed to replicate. A poetry collection to take home, to take to your heart." *Kevin P. Gilday, poet*

"Brave, lyrical and vivid." *Susan Burns, Chol Theatre*

"A steadying reminder of compassion in a world tipped off its axis." *Rosie Garland, poet & novelist*

"Work that refuses to accept half-baked assumptions, choosing instead to dig with precision to the roots of the world's ugliness." *Geneviève L. Walsh, spoken word artist*

"Dignity and strength underpin explorations of belonging, creativity and connection." *Ciarán Hodgers, spoken word artist*

"Wonderful, soothing and soulful. Her poetry is a friend when the world is a storm." *Louise Fazackerley, poet*

"Interesting, informative, amusing and poignant." *Edinburgh Fringe Review*

"Amazing, emotional poetry." *Emma Whitehall, writer & poet*

"Full of humanity and hope." *Rosie Fleeshman, spoken word artist*

"Global influences have helped shape a strong, grounded, and world-aware voice." *Dominic Berry, Glastonbury Poet in Residence 2017*

"Her subtle lyricism cradles you in a warm embrace and then gently but firmly delivers an emotional and thought-provoking gut punch." *Tina Sederholm, poet & performer*

"Uplifting and powerful." *Loud Poets*

"Thoughtful and clever." *Buxton Fringe Review*

"Her skill with words is deft and her message a reassuring embrace." *Alex Slater, poet & writer*

"An example of why we so desperately need to campaign for the survival of the arts." *Northern Soul*

ROSE CONDO

How to Find Where You Belong

Flapjack Press

flapjackpress.co.uk

Exploring the synergy between performance and the page

Published in 2023 by Flapjack Press
Salford, Gtr Manchester
🌐 flapjackpress.co.uk · **f** Flapjack Press
𝕏 flapjackpress · ▶ flapjackpress2520

ISBN 978-1-7396231-2-8

Printed by Imprint Digital
Exeter, Devon
🌐 digital.imprint.co.uk

FSC

MANCHESTER
A UNESCO City
of Literature

northern
fiction
alliance

Get out of my way
She said to her reflection
The mirror smiled back

Contents

Introduction

What were you doing twenty years ago? Were you an adult? A child? Unborn? Working? Studying? Learning to walk?

Twenty years ago, I moved to the UK for the first time. In 2003, I uprooted my life from the Canadian prairies to Edinburgh, Scotland. Fuelled by wanderlust, I leapt across the pond keen for travel and adventure.

I got lost a lot.

I got lost in Glasgow – repeatedly – thanks to performing in school shows in the days before SatNav.

I got lost in homesickness and loneliness, and ~~had to~~ have to confront social anxiety in order to make friends.

I got lost in relationships, and ~~had to~~ have to wrestle my voracious need to people please.

Through the highlights and hurdles of the past twenty years, I've used writing as a way of locating myself on the page. It's been a companion, a touchstone, a meaning-maker. It's led me to cross paths with people who have changed my life. It's brought connection, community, and very often a sense of belonging.

Belonging is fluid. It's not a fixed state of being. This book is less of a set of instructions, and more of a collection of reminders about how I might find where I belong.

My poems about place hold moments of the different locations I have called home. Years ago in an Edinburgh pub, my Scottish pal Malcolm read my palm. He spotted that the life line on my left hand is split into two. He said that part of my life might be split into two. He was right in ways that neither he nor I could have imagined.

For that, and for many reasons, my poems about place are split into two.

My poems about body navigate the work I do on feeling at home and safe in this tall, curvy collection of cells.

My poems about writing explore the comfort and familiarity I tend to find in the wordy shapes I make with my pen.

I hope you enjoy the journey through these poems. If you fancy connecting on the socials, perhaps take a selfie with the book and use the hashtag #rosecondofindwhereyoubelong.

Big love,
Rose x
September 2023

PLACE

(PART ONE)

Touching down:
arrival in Scotland, October 2003

Touching down
In a reality unknown
Spirited away
From memories sown
My day has come
Where the grass is green
My spirits soar
And my tears are clean
Innocence walking
In well-worn shoes
Miles lie ahead
And every day is new

Touching down
In a reality unknown
Thick with the stories
Of paradise grown
Voices of present
And past echo through
Beacons of light
In a sky white and blue
Innocence waking
From slumber of deep
New eyes behold
A world beyond sleep

Touching down
In a reality unknown
Where my feet are
Is where I call home

Sonnet 1995

Twenty years since you played the Danish prince
On a cold January prairie stage
Recalling your performance makes me wince
Your presence in the prairies caused a rage

Although you spoke the speech with tripping tongue
And sawed the air through less than skilful cries
Your struts and frets excited old and young
You struck stars in my adolescent eyes

It is with hindsight shame that you should know
That me my sister and her friend just might
Have lurked in my mom's car after the show
And chased you through the frozen winter night

Twenty years on what can I do but laugh
And somewhere I still have your autograph

6th April 2020

Ode to cooking for friends
I love the process from beginning to end
Planning the menu
Buying the food
Making a playlist
That sets the right mood
Sending out invites
And getting replies
Saying

> *Just bring yourself*
> *And some beer or some wine*

The day of the meal
I leap out of bed
Begin chopping and mixing
And prepping ahead
Sorting the starter
Readying the main
Making dessert
All to sustain
The appetites of
My dear friends
My guests
Hosting and cooking
Is what I love best
So when all this has passed
And we're en route to heal
Let's break bread together
C'mon by for a meal

Tribe

To those whose mere presence
Fully brightens my day
To those in whose eyes I see myself reflected
And think
Oh
Gosh
Actually
I'm pretty okay

You cheerleaders
You commiserators
We spill tea together
No matter the storms
The teacups
The weather

Whether minutes or months
Or decades have passed
Since we cackled or cried
Or raged or laughed

You are woven into the ways I can thrive
You are eternally
Collectively
Compassionately
My tribe

Snowflake

It was an average weekday
In the middle of May
I arrived home
Unlocked my door with my key
And there on the floor of my flat I see
A folded piece of paper
Had been slipped
Under the crack
The sight of this odd thing
Took me aback
I have an ex who is
A mad sociopath
He's sent me weird threatening
Stuff in the past
Here's me thinking
He's been in my building
Has defied the restraining order
With a trembling hand
I bent down to pick up
This folded page
With a feeling of dread
And this is 100% true
Is what the note said

> *Dear Tenant*
> *Can you kindly remove*
> *The paper snowflake decorations*
> *From your front windows*
> *Please note*
> *It is a breach of the lease*

To display anything
In the windows of the property
Kind regards
The Management

Um so right
I guess you could say
It was my oversight
Leaving up these
Offensive paper snowflakes
From December
Until the middle of May
Well beyond the traditional
Festive twelve days
Of a solstice-y mulled-wine scented season
But the reason The Management have written
Feels like the lamest of jokes
So I march to The Management's door
Convinced it was a hoax

Nope it's real

He stammered

I wrote it

He
Said the issue was raised
By the building's committee
Said the complaint had been
Officially submitted
Said displaying things in my window
Was not permitted

The average human lifespan is
Give or take
Seventy years
Which roughly equates to
Twenty-five thousand
Five hundred and fifty days
And it is very possible
To choose the ways
That we engage with
Communication and compassion
Seeking out ways to fashion our actions
To address injustices
To combat oppression
To acknowledge inequalities
To support self-expression

But as I peeled the
Provocative paper snowflakes
From my window
I tried to surmise
How this whimsy could cause
Such an assault on the eyes
Of someone whose sights
Were so set on despise
Someone whose life was perhaps
So dull so bland so free from strife
That complaining about my paper snowflakes
Was how they chose to live their life

This was the wrong in the world they needed to right
This was the dragon they needed to slay
This was the battle they chose to fight
Correcting my lease breach was their passageway

To moral vindication
By speaking to the committee

Well rest well citizens of all towns and cities
The scourge of outdated festive décor
Has been ripped from home windows
No more will your vision be plagued
By such damnable scrap
No more will you have to suffer
Such impertinent crap
Thank heavens this action has saved us
From enduring paper snowflakes
On the window of a private residence
In a Northern English town
Posted up by a Canadian
Who thought her nieces would enjoy them at Xmas
And then forgot to take them down
Long live this committee-reporting clown

As I folded my paper snowflakes into the bin
I did wonder
With a smirk
If this jerk realises that
Choosing to make
The entitled decision to take
Such unwarranted offense at my window decorations
Means they are the real
Snowflake

Just a bowl

It's a bowl
It's just a bowl
Red on the outside
White on the in
Chipped a bit on the rim
My fingers trace its curve
Recalling steamy soup stirred
Perfectly proportioned portions of porridge
There's plenty of use left in it to give
But this bowl is off to another home to live
About to be wrapped
And bound for a charity shop
This bowl
From a set I bought
Back before I met you
Back when
A bit broken
I began my life anew
Rebuilding
Resurrecting
My heart from the dead
This cheery cherry shade of red
Started to feature in all corners of my home
Reconnecting me to core courage
I'd always known
Red kettle
Red toaster
Red dishes to hold
Warmth and growth

Oh Rose

I sigh to myself

It's just a bowl

But this farewell
If I'm being honest and true
Is unexpectedly wistful
Which I say aloud to you
Despite myself I brace for a chiding
A scoff or a head shake
Or an eye roll deriding
My sentimentality
But you don't
And I remind myself
You've never done that to me

I get it

You say
And I know that you do
You smile and you say

That time meant a lot to you

You open your arms
Softly say

Come here

I smile and lean in
And blink away tears

The next day I drop off my donations
Including the red bowl
And in truth I don't mind
Knowing I now live in the heart
Of a partner who is kind

Box

I glance at it every morning
I've examined it closely once with mirrors
I try to keep it tidy
Maintaining its never-ending growth

It is nestled in my core
Between crossed legs and under belly flesh
It sits outside of their comfort zone
It lives in a space they are afraid to name

Haunted at times
Holding and releasing life blood in moon cycles
Holding power they fear as witchcraft
Holding depth of feminine wisdom

It carries a lineage
Of fierce determination
Though life has not passed through it
My box bears a pulse

Clumsmary

You said it with affection
A wry grin on your face
As I mopped up the tea
I'd spilled all over the place

> *You are like*
> *A baby gazelle*
> *The appearance of grace*
> *But a goofball as well*

Tripping and spilling
And stumbling and dropping
Are all things I do
I could work on stopping

I smash through most days
Like I'm in a race
Occasionally thinking
If I slowed my pace

I might be more mindful
Knock less things to the floor
But as I clear up the tea
What catches me more

Than my toe as I stub it
Walking past the bed
Is the manner in which
My nickname was said

You said it with affection
And I will be the butt of
Any joke that you make
In laughter and love

It's a sign of intelligence

Once upon a time I was a ballet dancer
This long-limbed lass donned pink tights
To pirouette
Plié
Sauté
Pas de bourée
Always aiming for poise and grace
But alas an imposter in pointe shoes
An adolescent growth spurt
Left ligaments loose and free
For injury
Less elegance
More elephant
A sign of intelligence
Someone recently said
As I recounted spilling sugar
All over the carpet at work
One of countless occurrences
Where I dropped
Tripped
Slipped
Spilled
Always aiming for poise and grace
But a sign of intelligence eh?
If that's the case
Then I must be
An absolute genius

Time travellers

Can we please go back in time
Relive rewind restart again
Through stolen nights from missing trains
I want to drink wine with you again
Outside locked up village stations
Under frozen starry constellations
My feet and fingers numb from cold
As you hold me sharing warmth in your embrace
I want to once again chase you through bedsheets
Tangle your limbs with mine
Let your fingers linger
At the ends of the lines you traced on my skin
Let's draw a roadmap back
To where we decided to begin

Did we decide to begin?

How did you suddenly
Take up so much space in me
Let's retrace can we
Relive rewind restart from the part
When coincidental journeys provided
Space where we found we collided
On common ground with shared reflection
And this new and simmering affection
Where possibility was abundant
And hope sprang unchecked
When we bedecked each other with kisses
Lips tasting curves
Breath on flesh

When my soul stirred
When my heart raced
I want to once again taste myself on your mouth
I want to once again carry your scent on me
I want to once again let hope spring eternally
Or at least linger again in the fantasy
That I temporarily held
Of you and me becoming an us
Before reality struck that it would never be thus

Can we please go back in time
Relive rewind restart again
For clearer ways to navigate
This beauty and this pain
Of seeing that our roads can't converge
Of seeing that our journeys won't ever merge
Of seeing that a fork lies in our path
Neither of us with a knife to carve and craft
A trail that we can travel together

Can I please go forward in time alone
To when I will have the wisdom to weather
How to let our longing fade
How to release you and be okay
Maybe one day
I'll see you and my knees won't go weak
I'll see you and won't go red in cheeks
I'll see you and be aloof and speak
Calm and wise and measured words
I've heard time heals so for now I'll believe

Eventually I'll stop feeling like I'm about to unravel
Eventually I'll stop wishing that we could time travel

Dear heart

Dear heart
Let me start
With I'm sorry
Sometimes I'm not very nice to you
As you beat endlessly
Pumping pleasure
Pain
Perseverance
Through me
Your rhythmic routine
The means by which I live
You give me breath and life
And how I wish you came with a user's guide
My core
Mon coeur
My power source
I get impatient when you ache
When you take ages to heal and grieve
I let you churn with anxiety
Carelessly leave you on my sleeve
I've given you away too fast and freely
And really
I must thank you
For being big and brave
Able to make me bold
So able to hold
Huge amounts of
Love
Compassion
And care

Dear heart
I swear
I will pay attention to your pounding
As signals sounding
Alerts to slow down
My expectations of what you can carry
To let go and let your power pulse through
Because I can only go on if you do too

Me and love

I am in love
With love
This noun
This verb
This full-figured word
Renders rose-tinted visions for me
With edges gently blurred
When I think on love
It's like all my senses awaken
It's like I've taken
A spoonful of thick chocolate pudding to my lips
Let the cool sweet ooze and drip onto my tongue
It's like every sound I hear is sung
As a sweet and lazy tune
It's like traffic noises croon
The manic panic of commuters
Is muted to a gentle hum
It's like warm waves of electricity
Emanate from every surface that I touch
It's like I feel a rush of anticipation
Whose energy sends me wishing to run
Leap twirl through cartwheels
To capture the rapture I feel
When I think on love

And love
Love loves to play games with me
Loves to play rounds of tag
Sending me chasing and racing after love's
Zig zag pattern
Laughingly darting from my grasp

Until feet pounding
Heart pounding
Rounding corners at full speed
I catch love in a corner and need
Only reach out with my fingertips
To whisper a breathless
Tag you're it

But it isn't all sunshine and roses
Me and love
We have our ups and downs
Love can be absent for long stretches
Love skips town
Slips down out of sight
And as I fight to find the corners
Where love languishes hidden
Meanwhile I get blindsided and bitten
By love's lookalikes
Love's doppelgangers
Love's wannabes

See
Sometimes lust dresses up like love
Sometimes attraction dresses up like love
Sometimes basic human decency dresses up like love
Sometimes fear dresses up like love
And sometimes the resemblance is so strong
That even though my deep inner knowing
Knows it's wrong I go along
Listening for every sound to be a song
Waiting to taste the chocolate pudding
Putting myself perfectly patiently placed
To feel an electric wave or spark
But I fumble and stumble around in the dark

Yet despite the absence of light
Once you know real love
You know when imitations just aren't right

And maybe I need to look closer
With less rose-tinted
Less fantasy-filled eyes
To see that love is still around
Just under a different guise
To hear love sung off the tongues of friends
To feel the love that's been sown
Into the family soil from which I've grown
And when I stumble and tumble through fear
That love won't ever really reappear
I reawaken my senses to see that love is always near

Hotline

Hello and thank you for calling the
'How to report an incident of sexual assault' hotline
We appreciate your time in taking this action
We want to ensure your call is not just a vengeful reaction
So before we put you through to someone to make your report
Our automated system will take you through a short
Series of questions

> To respond **Yes** press 1
> For **No** press **2**
> At the end we'll determine
> How best to put through
> Your call

Question One:

Do you have your story straight?
Can you clearly calculate every date and detail
Because if you fail to keep track of all that you've said
If your head clears after your current state
Of shock and trauma
And you remember more or different information later
It will only cause drama for you
And may lead authorities to question whether
Anything you said was true

Question Two:

Will you give us your name?
You may wish to remain anonymous
But what's easier for all of us
Is being able to track and trace

Whether this is your attempt to chase
Fame with your claim
False reporting happens
(Statistics suggest about 8% of the time
Which is the same amount of false reporting
For any other type of crime)

Question Three:
Are you upset enough?
Do you sound determined but not too tough?
Can you shed ample tears
To illustrate your real fears?
If you are too aloof you'll just seem lazy
But don't cry so much that you sound crazy

Question Four:
Look at what you are wearing
Now
Look down
Is this how you normally dress?
Does anything about your ensemble suggest
You regularly try to be alluring?
If you want this to be an enduring case
You may wish to consider covering everything but your face
If this case goes to court you'll want to purport to be a
Person of moral disposition
To lessen the suspicion
That you brought this on yourself

Question Five:
Think back on your behaviour and your attire
Prior to the alleged assault
Think carefully about these important details

Did your shoes or your clothes or your hair or your nails
Or your beverage choice or your level of intoxication
Or your volume of voice or your eye contact duration
Give any indication
That you were trying to entice sexual attention?
Could changes to these details
Have contributed to prevention?

Question Six:
We don't want to make assumptions
Though it is most often true
Was your alleged attacker male?
We'll need his name too

Question Seven:
Did you overreact?
Did you misunderstand
His hand on your knee
Or your chest or your breast or your thigh?
Is he just known as an affectionate guy?
Did you give him enough chances
To explain whether his advances
Were just playful and flirty?

Question Eight:
Have you ever sent him dirty
Photos or suggestive texting?
His defence will be hoping and expecting
That these messages occurred
These meanings get blurred
It will be your word against his
And your messages may present
Correspondence that communicates your consent

Question Nine:
Were you in a relationship with him that already existed?
Can you prove that you fought and resisted?
Can you convince a judge of the reasons that you stayed?
Can you prove that you tried and made
Every attempt to escape the situation?
If not your claim may be without foundation

Question Ten:
Do you accept that the burden of proof won't lie with him?
That his defence will only seek pins
To poke enough holes in your story
To let your credibility seep out
So that he can be found not guilty
By reasonable doubt

This brings us to the end of our questions
We'll use your responses as a guide
To help us decide your level of need

Careful analysis of your answers
Tells us your case is unlikely to succeed
Therefore your call will not proceed
There are no further options at this point to try
Thank you for calling
Better luck next time
Goodbye

England & Wales: rapecrisis.org.uk
Scotland: rapecrisisscotland.org.uk
Ireland: rcni.ie
Europe: rcne.com

For a woman

He is an uncomfortably close talker
Oblivious to the concept of personal space
I stand awkwardly too timid or intimidated
To meet his face and ask him to step back a bit
I stand silently and wish that it
Wasn't something I found so hard to do
I don't want to appear to be rude
I suck on that sour irony as his lewd
Leaning continues through
The discussion he's having
About an artist we both know
I am so in awe of the person he refers to
I try to inject my views into this
One way conversation
But get stuck in preoccupation
With bracing myself against his hot breath
And vocal volume that's starting to swell
And then he leans in even closer
To proclaim

> *Yes she's done very well*
> *Especially*
> *For a woman*

Is it possible for one's ovaries to boil?
Because if so then mine did
In outraged turmoil
Because comments like this that
Keep the cultivation of soil
Fresh and fertile for intolerance to grow

As though people who identify
As anything outside
Of cis straight male
Somehow fail or run at a loss
As though there is a cost
To overcome by being deemed as less
As though a single identity is the
Benchmark for success
Comments like that
Are counter-productive
And ultimately reductive
'For a woman'
Nor is there a way
For the tables to be turned
For him to aim to earn
Such an accolade
Merely made
On the basis the way in which he
Sees a narrow gender binary

But I don't say any of this

I just sigh
Close my eyes
Give a slight smile and nod
Feeling like an utter fraud
In the heat of his hot breath
I was not outspoken
My voice too timid or intimidated and choked
To challenge his narrow perspective
Instead I stood silently ineffective
I cannot abide feeling this pathetic and perverse

So inside this echo chamber
I want to try to rehearse
To prepare empowered air into my lungs
Ready with resistant words on my lips and tongue
So that when hot-breath-close-talkers
Utter such words again one day
I might be more ready
To more confidently say

> *For a woman you say*
> *When people use this phrase*
> *I do not think it means what they think it means*
> *Gender identity is not some worth-defining scheme*
> *What you said is reductive and offensive*

And hot-breath-close-talkers may get defensive
But that's not for me to manage or soothe
And it may prompt them to use
Language more conducive
To being inclusive across a broader gender range
And I might say it quietly and not shout
But at least I'll speak up and speak out
Towards change

Today I will

Today I will look at myself
With kindness
Or at least I will try
My lenses need cleaning
Need to wipe away smudges that blur
Smeared on by a system
Set up to ensure
I hate what I see

Today I will be
In the space that I take up
Try to give fewer fucks
About how perceptions of me land
Feel less apologetic for how I
Move
Exist
Speak
Stand
Fuel forgiveness in myself
For ongoing fears about my size

Today I will realise
That the determining male gaze
Also lives within my eyes
Marring my view with grit
And guilt
And shame
And grist
Don't I call myself a feminist

Today I will resist
Holding my handbag
In front of my midsection when I sit
Accept that no-one actually gives a shit
Occupy my mind
With outer considerations
Open up space for
So many other observations

Today I will forego
Feeling like a flake
For the amount of effort I take
In denying my desire to people please
In releasing my resentment
Towards those who have ease
In their bodies
In their voices
In their passions
In their choices
I will note that no matter what
Others are pursuing
Nobody really knows what they are doing
Any more or less than me

The day after that
I will look at myself
With kindness
Or at least I will try

Raising words

The café clatters with noise / Chatter of patrons / Parents with prams / She sits in a corner and tends her words / Not an infant but a page crying for her attention / She nurses this call / Cradling her pen as words pour from the nib / Stroking her notebook with gentle patience / Something new is being created in her hands / For a moment she and her words are one / Nothing else matters in the world

A tiny hand on her knee stirs this reverie / A cookie-crumbed face looks up at her wide-eyed / Sorry says a breathless parent / I'd only looked away for a moment / It's okay she says / The parent smiles then sniffs the air / Someone needs a change / In a swoop whisks the child away

She decides to call it a day / To let her words rest a while / She scans her fledgling ideas with a look that says / Don't worry I'll soon return / Folds her notebook closed / Tucks it gently into her rucksack / She carries the weight of her newborn composition proudly on her back / As she approaches the exit she spies the same parent / Grappling with pram and door / She holds it open / The breathless parent says / Hi sorry thank you / And with their beloved creations / Both head out

The language of ducks:
scene from a grade 3 classroom in Winnipeg circa 1985

Ducks don't speak!

He bellowed

You should know that by now!

Her cheeks flushed
Her heart sped
He'd said
Circle the ones that are not true
She'd studied her worksheet
A few drawings of scenarios
Her thoughtful considered mind
Paused before she chose

A drawing of someone
With fingers made of bubble gum
She confidently circled
That was silly and dumb

A cloud raining carrots from above
She circled it and she knew
This illustration
Definitely was not true

She left uncircled
A dog on a leash
A bus and its driver
A picnic on a beach

The final image
A group of ducks
One wore a kerchief
Tied and tucked
Under her bill
And a speech bubble said
Come along my ducklings
It's straight home to bed
She left it uncircled
Handed her sheet in
And later in the day
She met the din
Of his sneers and laughs
As he barked out her error
In front of the class

Ducks don't speak!

How could she have allowed
Herself such a blunder
Yet after a moment
From under the shame
She felt a flame of indignance
Start to flicker and grow
Ducks don't speak
How does he know

Sure she'd never seen
A duck wear a 'kerchief
But deep down
She was sure that
What she saw on the sheet
Was a cartoon translation

Of the quacking and clucks
Shared between ducks

A young mind such as hers
Had not yet learned the words
To speak up and speak out
Against what he had to say
Nevertheless
Her conviction about the language of ducks
Is something she still believes today

Give me a script

(lights up)

Give me a script / Weave words for me /
That I can use to rip / And roar / And soar
to intellectual heights / Inciting inspiration
/ With ease and muster and might

(pause)

Give me a script / Solid and sound / That
will pull no punches / And pound out /
Exactly what I mean / No need to read
between / My lines of reason / Will suit
any season / No scenario / Will know / Of
my tongue tied in knots / I will not be at a
loss / Words will be plentiful / And not
wasted / Gesticulating / But spent artfully /
Articulating

(pause)

Give me a script / That I may / Renounce
the day / I would ever again be pounced
on / As you prey / On my not knowing
what to say / Pounced on / As you prey /
On the places / Where I need the spaces /
To pause and place and space / My
thoughts / While all the while / My tongue
ties in knots / Tangled in the web you
weave / To verbally bully me / Leaving me
/ Ripped and stripped / And gripped / In
feeling ill-equipped / And wishing / That
someone / Somewhere / Would please give
me a script

(lights down)

Ellipses and exclamations

It is because I was a theatre kid
Fond of pauses ... and proclamations!

It is because I write as I see the world
Making space for joy ... and appreciations!

It is because of my rampant enthusiasm
Broadcasting awe ... and admirations!

It is because of my love of language
For connection ... and communications!

It is because creativity has power
For confidence ... and innovations!

It is because I eschew grammar rules
Defying structure ... and limitations!

It is because speaking up takes courage
Through resistance ... and protestations!

Therefore
I will perpetually pepper my phrases
With ellipses ... and exclamations!

Bake Off dreams

Recently I dreamt
I was competing in the big white tent
Yes me in my dream I had set off
As a contestant on *The Great British Bake Off*

I had silly banter with Alison and with Noel
They loved the way I could kid and cajole

> *Guys*

I said

> *I'll fill my cakes with booze*
> *Because apparently that helps to gain Prue's approval*

I managed to disarm
Paul Hollywood with my Canadian charm

> *Paul*

I said

> *How's it going eh hosehead*
> *There's no doubt about it you've never seen*
> *A dish as delish as my poutine*

Beyond my endearing Canadian cheek
I wowed with my words every week
My poetry stirred Paul's steely glare
My cupcakes and couplets were crafted with care

In biscuit week my rhymes had such snap
The other bakers cheered and clapped

My pastry phrases formed a sumptuous gallery
And Prue declared them worth every calorie

Were proving drawers a home for my bread week dough
Fie and forsooth and forget it oh no
My bread burst forth balladry that was baked just enough
Rhymes rolled from me more layered than rough puff

The luscious lines of my signature bake
So inspired Paul that he spake
A haiku while giving me a Hollywood handshake

Each technical challenge of the baking bonanza
I created as an exemplary stanza
In my triumphant opus – my GBBO delight
And there was ne'er a soggy bottom in sight

Each of my poetic showstopper creations
Cultivated culinary ovations
I wowed in every single *Bake Off* task

> *But Rose*
> *Can you actually bake*
> *Like in real life*

I hear you ask

See here's the thing
I can bake pretty well
But my skills are pretty basic
No Creme Caramel
No Florentines or Roulades
No Ciabatta or Focaccia
No Baklava or Mille-Feuille
I have a plan
See here's the catch yeah

I just need poetry to give me a little bit of fame
Not huge superstardom but just enough acclaim
To get me an invite
A sneaky inroad
For me to wow with my words on a special celebrity episode
A one-off where I wouldn't need baking abilities supreme
But in the meantime
I guess I'll have to win *The Great British Bake Off* in my dreams

Look up

Look up how to be a freelance poet
Look up how to register as self-employed
Look up how to do self-employment taxes
Look up poetry events to attend
Look up poetry promoters to contact
Look up poets to follow
Look up trending hashtags
Look up inspiring Ted Talks
Look up notable women in history
Look up the top ten films to see before you die
Look up the top ten books to read before you die
Look up the top ten places to visit before you die
Look up what to do when you die

Look up writing a will
Look up making a retirement plan
Look up making a ten-year plan
Look up making a five-year plan
Look up the weather for next week

Look up how to be more confident
Look up how to be less insecure
Look up how to be more present
Look up how to be less anxious
Look up how to tell if depression is hereditary

Look up how to play a ukulele
Look up how to tune a ukulele
Look up Bruno Mars songs
Look up a crush from high school
Look up past boyfriends
Look up current friends on holiday

Look up training for a 10k
Look up yoga retreats
Look up meditation practices
Look up vegan recipes
Look up volunteering opportunities
Look up human rights organisations
Look up online petitions to sign
Look up socialism
Look up activism
Look up minimalism
Look up how to build a tiny house

Look up current bank balance
Look up current credit card balance
Look up last minute flight prices
Look up car hire prices
Look up Airbnb options in Berlin
Look up second hand bicycles for sale
Look up how to build a garden compost bin

Look up being gluten free
Look up being dairy free
Look up being alcohol free
Look up being medication free
Look up being debt free
Look up being doubt free
Look up being distraction free
Look up being technology free
Look up being anxiety free
Look up being envy free
Look up being free
Look up being
Look up

Waiting

When

>*The pen asked*
>*Sitting idle on a page*

When will she use us to write you down
It's been an age

Have patience

>*The ideas said*

The day will come when her head
Will be flooded with us
In such a gush
She will grab you and rush
To write all of us down
Before we fly out of her head
The time will come

>*The ideas said*

Have patience

But how

>*The pen asked*

Can I compete
With all the tasks
Stress and deadlines
She tries to meet

What about

The pen asked

The way she distracts
Herself with podcasts and playlists
Noise at every turn

I hear you

The ideas said

Look we try to burn
Bright enough in her mind
To force her to come and find you
And scratch us down before we fade

Then why

The pen asked

Hasn't she made
The time to use us
I know she can do it
She's done it before
I'm hardly mightier than a sword
Sitting here ignored
Can't you do more
Burn brighter
Strike harder
Smack her upside the head

Have patience

The ideas said

We know it is tough
We are confident at some point
She will miss us enough
That she'll set aside deadlines and tasks
She'll pause distractions and podcasts
And notice us
Notice what we ignite
Then find you
Find paper
She will write
Once more
She will do it again
Until then
My pen friend
We must remain
At the ready
Ever present
It will be worth the wait
When we three in unity
Come together to create

RhymeZone

I have to own up about a growing affliction
It's becoming a habit
Could soon be an addiction
Can I say the words out loud
The shame cuts deep to the bone
My name is Rose Condo and I use RhymeZone

In case you haven't heard of Rhyme Zone
It is an online rhyming dictionary
I tell myself it's cheating
I tell myself I'm very
Bad
Sad
Mad
Not glad or rad
And more than just a tad pathetic

I tell myself using RhymeZone makes me a poet fraud
Which triggers self-loathing
I know that sounds odd
About how anxious using a rhyming dictionary makes me
But then I get caught in a wave of anxieties that takes me
Sometimes close to the edge of a worrying abyss
Replaying moments to the point of paralysis
Spinning in spirals of dizzying analysis
Declaring I should have known better than
Doing what I did
It would be better if I just hid behind
The pretence that I'm fine
Just a bit stressed

No matter no mind
Find
Bind
Rewind
Remind
Remind myself I have tools for this
Ways to edge away from the
Edge of the abyss
I could make a list
Of some of things that make me anxious
Feeling like a fraud for using Rhyme Zone
The fact that nothing rhymes with anxious

Telling someone I like them
Walking home alone at night
Never being thin enough
Hairy bugs that bite

Worry that I'm too sensitive
And take things too much to heart
Worry that when I've eaten lentils
I'll forget myself and fart

Being at a social gathering
Where I don't know anyone
Worry that I'm too serious
And don't have enough fun

Guilt that I don't do enough
To help others in need
Guilt that my first world world
Is built on gluttony and greed

Worry that I don't read the right books
Or listen to the right songs
Fear that I'm a disappointment
Fear that I'm doing it all wrong

Fear of getting cancer
Fear of loved ones dying
Fear of being alone forever
Fear that time is flying

Okay I say
Stopping there to look at my list
Resisting shame and guilt and regret
As I try not to let these anxieties churn and seethe
As I try to breathe back to presence and place
With a lens of grace and a new way of seeing
That it's okay to be okay with being
Exquisitely imperfectly human and flawed
That using RhymeZone doesn't make me a poet fraud
That speaking up helps anxieties to ease
More trees
More bees
More compassionate sharing please

I don't have time

I don't have time to write this poem
Because my books aren't going to alphabetize themselves
Because my spices aren't going to alphabetize themselves
Because Instagram won't check itself
Because Wordle won't solve itself
Because I need to update my LinkedIn
Because I need to consider leaving social media
Because I secretly love my social media spiral

I don't have time to write this poem
Because it won't be good enough to go viral
Because it will never win a slam
Because it will be too short
Because it will be too long
Because it will be too obvious
Because I am too obvious
Because who really cares what I have to say

I don't have time to write this poem
Because I should do this online survey
Because I should text my mum
Because I should find a good yoga video
Because I should be doing kegels
Because I should count the days since my last period
To gauge where I am in my cycle
To see if that explains why I cried for two hours yesterday

I don't have time to write this poem
Because I want to punch this stupid poem in its dickhead face
Because I'm so tired
Because I'm too tired
Because I'm really fucking tired

to write this poem

I don't have time to write this poem
Because the world is on fire
Because the country is in shambles
Because corruption
Because racism
Because poverty
Because austerity
Because inequality
Because misogyny
Because transphobia

Because it will only land in an echo chamber

Because it will only land in an echo chamber

Because it will only land in an echo chamber

Because it will only land in an echo chamber

Because it will only land in an echo chamber

Because it will only land in an echo chamber

Because it will only land in an echo chamber

Because it will only land in an echo chamber

Because it will only land in an echo chamber

Because it will only land in an echo chamber

Because it will only land in an echo chamber

Because it will only land in an echo chamber

Because it will only land in an echo chamber

Because it will only land in an echo chamber

Because it will only land in an echo chamber

Because it will only land in an echo chamber

Because it will only land in an echo chamber

Just

Just	*saying*
Just	*enough*
Just	*to say*
Just	*a minute*
Just	*a sec*
Just	*a little bit*
Just	*a little bit more*
Just	*a gentle reminder*
Just	*don't*
Just	*go*
Just	*asking*
Just	*stay*

~~just~~	Saying
~~just~~	Enough
~~just~~	To say
~~just~~	A minute
~~just~~	A sec
~~just~~	A little bit
~~just~~	A little bit more
~~just~~	A gentle reminder
~~just~~	Don't
~~just~~	Go
~~just~~	Asking
~~just~~	Stay

PLACE

(PART TWO)

My Winnipeg

I'm always the one
To make the trip across the pond
I know you can't visit
I know I am fond
Of mentioning you
Often
I'll say

> *And this one time*
> *In Winnipeg*

Over pints I drop names of your progeny

> *Hey guess which singer went to the same*
> *High school as me*
> *And did you know*
> *An orphaned bear cub at Winnipeg's Zoo*
> *Inspired the story of Winnie the Pooh*

I tell tales of how cold you get
Smugly watching jaws drop but I forget
The ferocity felt as your windchill climbs
I hold you fixed and keep you frozen in time

I still call you home
My prairie roots hold strong
When foreign lands feel unsettled
You are where my beginnings belong

You hold many of my firsts
Kiss, sex, hangover, heartbreak

First car, first flat on my own
Your muddy waters make

Rivers of remembering in me
They freeze and thaw and flow
They fork at points of perspective
That nourished soil for me to grow

Though your soil is in truth
Treaty One Territory
Traditional home of the Anishnaabe
Cree, Dakota, Dene and Métis

To one great city
From a little prairie town
My childhood moved to Charleswood
Then to River Heights then downtown

You are where I cut
My cultural teeth
Royal Winnipeg Ballet
RMTC
Winnipeg Fringe
Rainbow Stage
Manitoba Theatre for Young People
Prairie Theatre Exchange
Your thriving hub of Canadian arts
Still pulses strong in my prairie heart

Your culinary delights
Are things I still crave
Salivating about Slurpees
Half cola half grape

You were never great for a pub crawl
Places spread too far along winter roads
So I cocooned with Celtic tunes
Sung and played at The Toad

This prairie rose's roots
I have transplanted her
To Edinburgh
To Leeds
And now to Manchester
But I still call you home
Is that okay?
Is there a statute of limitations
Based on how long I've been away

One great city
I know you're not without your faults
I know many in your midst
Live in desperate need or want
I know many of the citizens
Of your flat grid streets
Work hard to try and serve
Your community's needs

When I visit part of me
Doesn't want you to have changed
But you needed to and also
I haven't stayed the same

Will we recognise each other
Winnipeg
When I land
Now older
Now married

Now here with a man
Who is encountering your features
With eyes fresh and new
My Winnipeg
My love
Please be good to him too

Sounds of your city

You sing me the sounds of your city
I settle in and Sit Down
In Our House
All Uncovered
To hear of your Dirty Old Town

Guess Who led me to say
This Feels Like Home
This Charming Man
With your Heart of Gold

Half a World Away
I was too Neil Young
To know One Day Like This
Would eventually come

Leaving was a
Bittersweet Symphony
I miss the Harvest Moon
That rose over One Great City

But no Blue Monday
Only Happy Mondays ahead
As I trade my prairie roses
For your Stone Roses instead

These Eyes make me Weakerthan
An Elbow to my heart
Only Joy no Division
Love Will Never Tear Us Apart

Because you sing me the sounds of your city
An Oasis of an adopted home
To 24 Hour Party People
Immortalised in song
And Someday You Will Find Me
Learning to sing along

Lockdown Lock-in

The Rose and Crown
Was what we'd called the kitchen
The bedroom
The Boudoir
The bathroom
The Porcelain Throne
Pub names we created on our own
Hand-drawn signs hung with bits of blu-tack
On magnolia-painted doors in our little flat
The distance between pubs
Wasn't too far
No overpriced pints
No waiting at the bar
No blaring tunes
To drown out our chat
No bumping into pals
No Charlie the cat
No banter with a bouncer
No waiting in queues
I didn't wear a bra
You didn't wear shoes

Spider

The elevator was going up
A movement she hoped
Would help lift her mood
Help ease the weight
Of the pack on her back

     You look prepared

Said the man stood next to her

     You've got it all in there
     Brolly
     Bottle of water
     Everything

She half smiled
Half heard him
Half wished she could swap spots
With the eight-legged arthropod she saw
Crawling up the metal door
Carrying all it needed
Everything

Oh she thought
Watching it ascend to the ceiling
That feeling of climbing to any height
To set sights through eight eyes
On where to web up for the night
To weave a home anywhere she liked
To patiently craft her means to catch
Prey for her meal

Not wanting to feast on flies
She could yet feel a kinship
Longing for her own arachnid days

Her gaze blinked back into focus
As the elevator doors slid open

> *Is this your floor*

He asked

> *No*

She said

> *I'm up one more*

> *Your accent*

He said as he stepped out

> *Where are you from*

> *I travel around a lot*

She said

> *I'm a writer*

As the doors slid closed
She smiled realising
How closely that rhymes with spider

Dear Evidently

Dear Evidently
How can I put into words what you meant to me

You were run by a terrifically talented trio
You provided a monthly dose of Haribo

You were a place where so many friendships were forged
You were a bargain at a mere three pounds on the door

You were – to me and many – the best spoken word night
You brought the best of the best to Salford
(which is a Broadway musical right?)

You brought the chance to cross paths with
Liv Barnes, Ella Gainsborough and Kieren King
You were – for me – completely life-altering

You taught me how to climb up and through imposter syndrome
You made The Eagle a beautiful spoken word home

Your radio show, slams, videos and anthologies
Bring up an extra special thanks from me

For giving me confidence and courage to pursue this poetry path

For the guaranteed monthly hugs, words and laughs
For being there when my bruised soul needed to be filled
For being a place where my broken spirit could rebuild

Your groovy gatherings now live in memory
But the second Monday of the month will eternally
Bring echoes of you

Concluded but never gone
Evidently
In hearts and artists
You live on

How to find where you belong

How to find where you belong

Leave

Leave where you are
Leave where you are living
Whether that's in a city
Or an apartment
Or an awkward uncomfortable place in your heart

Whether your departure is expected
Or unplanned
Understand
That where you are leaving
May not be there for you to return to one day to live

Pack possessions that matter
Pack perspectives that matter
Try to leave behind the ones that don't
Try to embrace that you won't love
Every part of the leaving

Try to pack light
You can't carry everything
The handmade Christmas stocking
Posters from your very first flat
Shoeboxes of photographs
If you leave these things behind
Because you need to leave in haste
Know some things can be replaced
And what can't will always hold space within you

Feel excited and delighted by pastures new
Navigate new faces and places
Greetings and goodbyes
Some people
The saying goes
Come into our lives
Forever or for a season
Whatever the reason
Keep going
Notice and feel grateful for when the path is smooth
Keep going
You'll stumble when the path gets rough
Keep going
It just helps the skin on your feet to get tough
Keep going

Except for when you need to break
For when sorrow and heartache
Catch up with you
Disrupting you with a need to grieve
Some of what you had to leave

This grief may grip you
Stronger than you would wish
It may squeeze air and aspiration from you
It may drain desire and feel like it will never let go

Know that you have strength and grace to face it
And if you stop and sit and wait
Your lungs will remember how to reinflate
Your hands will remember how to push yourself up
Your feet will remember how to step one in front of the other
Your fingers will remember how to brush
Crusts of salted sadness and sleep from your eyes

So rest
Catch your breath
Then rise again

Keep going
Take care
Keep going
Take it steady

And when something somewhere decides you are ready
A destination will appear
Warm and welcoming
Glowing from the inside out
And a voice of doubt
Insidious and insistent
Will whisper in your ear
All the reasons you tell yourself
You are wrong here
You don't belong here
Face those thoughts
Replace those thoughts
Be bold

See someone hold the entrance open
Trust their welcoming beckon
Reckon you've made it this far
It's worth stepping in and stopping in for a bit
And despite being new to you it's likely this place
Will feel somehow familiar too
So much so that you set down your load
Let yourself settle into this new abode
Because here lies
Community
Friendship

All you didn't know you need
All the ways to nourish and feed
Your body and spirit and mind

And in time that might be an instant
Or in time that might be tentative and long
In time let yourself believe
That you have found where you belong

Acknowledgements

Which came first – the joy of arrival or the gratitude to everyone who supported the journey? I couldn't have done either without these folks:

Mom, Dad, Heather, Graham, Tanya, Sue, Abi, Sadie, Dave, Jess, Nolan, Ben, Paul, Jayne and Emma.
My family. My fabric.

Andrea, Ann, Barb, Barry, Chris, Ciarán, Claire B, Claire H, Dri, Ella, Ellie, Erin, Gen, Helen, Jake, Jen, Jenny, Kat, Laura, Maggie, Neil, Rana, Ray, Sameena, Simon, Tina, Tom, Tony.
My tribe.

Arts Emergency team, Attic Stories crew, Flapjack crew, Flat Iron Choir, hoot creative arts, Huddersfield Literature Festival, Lawrence Batley Theatre, Manitoba Theatre for Young People, Prairie Theatre Exchange, U of W Theatre and Drama class of 2000.
My cultural cultivators.

Kieren.
My best.

You.
My reason.